30 Day ESSENTIALS for MARRIAGE

3o Day ESSENTIALS for

MARRIAGE

JYOTISH NOVAK

CRYSTAL CLARITY PUBLISHERS
NEVADA CITY, CALIFORNIA

Copyright © 2002 by Crystal Clarity Publishers
All rights reserved
ISBN 1-56589-168-6
1 3 5 7 9 10 8 6 4 2

Design by Stephanie Steyer and C.A. Starner Schuppe
Photography by Swami Kriyananda, Jyotish Novak,
     Barbara Bingham and Stephanie Steyer

Crystal Clarity Publishers
14618 Tyler-Foote Road
Nevada City, CA 95959

Phone: 800 424-1055 or 530 478-7600
E-mail: clarity@crystalclarity.com
Website: www.crystalclarity.com

Library of Congress CIP data available

Printed in China

This book is dedicated, in gratitude, to my great
teachers who have taught me more about life and values
than I can ever say.

And to my wife who has shown me what a
blessing and joy marriage can be.

For most people marriage is a source of great fulfillment and yet, for many of us, sharing a life with a partner can present challenges. Whether your relationship is easy or difficult, the 30 *Day Essentials for Marriage* can help you improve your life together.

For those just starting a marriage, it is important to establish good patterns right away. A new marriage, like a young plant, can be trained and molded. The 30 *Day Essentials for Marriage* will help you establish those qualities and habits that will make your life together happy and fulfilling.

Those who have been married for some time need ways to keep their relationship from growing stale and routine. This book will be a road map into areas you may not have gone before.

Spend a few minutes reading through this book to get an idea of where you are heading. Then, take one day at a time and work on the quality for that day. You may want to stay with one quality for a longer time or return later to develop it further. Each day ends with a simple, concrete "action" item. Try them!

While an individual can use it, the book is designed to be a way for couples to work together. Merely reading it together can be a great help for you and your partner. But if you actually use it as a guide it can transform your life together. It is simple and fun. But the effects can be profound.

1

Have Fun

Having fun together is vital for a happy marriage. Every day should include some merriment. Run, dance, joke — do something simply for the joy of it. A joyful mind will help you feel physically and mentally healthy. And joy will make your marriage healthy too. The force of gravity can collapse bridges and buildings. Over time, a relationship can collapse from the pressures of stress, disappointment and self-involvement. Couples need to counter the force of gravity with the law of "levity." You don't want to become like one of those couples sitting grimly and silently at a restaurant table. They've lost their levity, their ability to have fun. Keep your marriage living and growing by finding new ways to laugh and play together. Start now! Never stop!

TRY THIS

Ask each other,
"What should we
do today just for the
fun of it?"

TRY THIS

Take a walk. Hold hands and enjoy the moment
with your dearest friend.

Be Friends

Make friendship the foundation for your relationship. Wise counselors and scientific studies tell us that those marriages that are based on friendship survive the tests of time. We choose our friends for the simple pleasure of being together. True friends don't always have to agree; that would be too boring. But even when their opinions differ, friends still radiate a sense of quiet support. Make your partner your best friend. Think back about what drew you together and be sure to keep those feelings alive. Visualize holding hands with your loved one, walking, talking, and laughing together. Now visualize this happening on the day of your 50th anniversary. With friendship as your first priority your marriage will ride above all life's storms.

DAY 3

TRY THIS

Have a

conversation

about something

important

to you.

Develop Your
Communication

Rapport between a couple is built by good communication. Without it you'll be like islands, separate and alone, and misunderstandings will inevitably occur. Good communication is a skill that can be developed. Start by really paying attention to your partner, listening and watching for what is being expressed beneath the surface. Conversation will deepen only when there is a sense of trust and security. Don't criticize or belittle your partner if you want them to open up to you. Trust develops when you express support and appreciation. Men and women communicate differently, a cause of endless amusement and frustration in society. Most men need to improve their ability to express their feelings. Women need to appreciate men's non-verbal messages, to understand that men show love by actions and not only words. Find a time today, and every day, to have at least one genuine conversation, one where you really talk and really listen.

Express Appreciation

Appreciation in a marriage is like sunlight in a garden. It helps the blossoms of your love grow strong and healthy. Tell your partner, today, something that you appreciate about him or her. Then make this a daily habit. Avoid, like poison, the tendency to criticize your companion. Criticism makes people defensive and delays the very changes you want to see. Instead, look to his positive qualities and give him appreciation and encouragement. People, like plants, grow when they are nurtured. One of life's hidden laws is that we get back what we give out. By expressing appreciation for your loved ones, you open the channel for them to express the same for you. If you and your partner develop the simple habit of expressing appreciation, your marriage will take on a golden glow of harmony.

DAY

4

TRY THIS

Tell your partner

three things that

you most

appreciate about

him or her.

D A Y 5

TRY THIS

Before you go to sleep, review the day.

Accept responsibility for every action, thought, and mood.

Affirm, "I am happy in myself."

Take Responsibility
for Yourself

Take responsibility for yourself, for your actions, moods and state of mind. You alone are responsible for your happiness. Don't blame others for your troubles. Life is a series of lessons and, in fact, we draw to ourselves exactly the people and circumstances we need for our growth. A wise man said, "Conditions are always neutral, it is how we react to them that makes them seem good or bad." You can't always control what happens but you can control your reactions. Start by accepting complete responsibility for your life. Then you can begin to make necessary changes. Don't expect your partner to make you happy nor allow what he or she does to make you unhappy. Realize that only you, not the world around you, create your good or bad moods. Then decide, simply, to be happy under all circumstances.

A giving
heart not only
expresses love
but also draws
it from others.

TRY THIS

Talk together
and then make
intelligent decisions
about habits that
influence your
health.

Health

Your health, good or bad, will be an important part of your life together. There are a few simple habits that will have a profound effect on your long-term health and vitality. Now is the time to establish healthy habits. First, since you and your partner will be having most of your meals together, discuss the foods you eat and make sure that your diet is a healthy one. Vitality comes with fresh fruits and vegetables while processed foods, meat and junk food gradually erode your well-being. Look also at your exercise patterns and try to build into each day at least a half-hour of vigorous activity. Make sure you get enough but not too much sleep. And, finally, avoid the three addictions that will be disastrous over the long run – smoking, using drugs, and excessive use of alcohol. Remember, your partner and your children will share the results of your decisions about such things. Choose to be healthy.

Inner Strength

Be your own person. Don't try to mold yourself to fit an image others might hold. Inner strength increases as you develop your natural talents and trust your own ideas. Work with strengths that you have already. What is your best asset? Is it your intellect, your creativity, your ability to work hard? Your talents are your true treasure. Inner strength is like the trunk of a tree, everything else branches out from it. Don't allow the opinions of others to push you around. Let them wash past you as a stream flows around a stone. Yet at the same time, the strong person listens carefully to the messages life is trying to send. When you are calm and centered you will be able to perceive truth as it resonates within you. Then, from a position of inner strength you can follow the best course of action. One of the greatest benefits of a strong marriage is having the constant support of a loved one. If you each encourage your partner to develop inner strength, your marriage will grow strong and dynamic.

DAY 7

TRY THIS

Sit with your partner
and explore together
what makes each of
you strong.
Agree mutually to
support those qualities
in all circumstances.

The Power of
Positive Energy

Positive energy is like the switch for a light. Turn it on and energy flows; turn it off and you stumble around in the dark. The first step to a fulfilling marriage is to make sure you have a strong flow of positive energy and enthusiasm. Start by being enthusiastic about things you already enjoy doing together. When this habit is strongly ingrained it will become second nature to be more positive about even those tasks you find tedious or unpleasant. Positive energy is a powerful force for overcoming problems of all kinds. The first step to accomplishing anything, be it doing a project or overcoming a mood, is to get energy flowing. When you're stuck, actions are better than words. Do something physical for a few minutes; take a walk or do some deep breathing. Get your blood flowing and your thoughts will start to flow too. As a wise man said, "Act enthusiastic and you'll be enthusiastic."

DAY 8

TRY THIS

Do

something

together

and do it

with

enthusiasm.

DAY

9

TRY THIS

Think, with respect, about the deep soul-qualities of your partner.

Respect
Your Partner

Respect for your partner is one of the cornerstones of marriage. Don't take your partner for granted. Look to the deeper nature of your loved one, to the soul qualities, and give that your deepest respect. Remember that both you and your partner have a right to your own thoughts and opinions. Respect your loved one's independence and don't over-emphasize trivial differences. Even when you disagree, reassure your partner that, though you might differ, you still love and respect them. Often disagreements arise, not because the actual topic is important, but because one or both partners feel that their opinions are being ignored. Strong marriages develop a balance between intimacy and space, between presumption and respect. A strong marriage also needs time for each partner to be quiet and inward. Respect for your partner means also that you should never belittle him or her in front of others, especially your children. Respect and love grow from the same root.

TRY THIS

Watch carefully
your emotional
reactions to events.
As soon as you observe
an unwanted reaction,
resolve to be
even-minded
and cheerful
in all
circumstances.

Even-Mindedness

Even-mindedness is one of the most important attitudes you can develop not only for marriage, but also for life in general. Emotions are like waves, rising and crashing. Don't let emotional storms toss you around — it is hard on you and hard on your partner. Feelings, even when communicated only in subtle ways, create an emotional environment in which your marriage must live. If you allow moods to run wild they will give your loved-one a case of emotional whiplash. To develop even-mindedness simply accept conditions and people just as they are. Take a longer view of life and its challenges. Realize that emotional outbursts have the power to destroy a relationship. Calm their destructive storms with the sunshine of even-mindedness. The key to happiness is to always be even-minded and cheerful.

Look to the deeper nature of your loved one, to the soul qualities, and give that your deepest respect.

Have Realistic
Expectations

Most of life's disappointments are caused by unrealistic expectations. A recent study shows that the root-cause of bad moods is the accumulation of many small disappointments. Don't expect the world to make you happy. Having realistic expectations helps you maintain a positive opinion and is especially important in a marriage and family. Being disappointed because your partner doesn't quite measure up creates frustration and friction. If your expectations are so lofty that your partner can never please you, he will feel a sense of failure, impotence and hopelessness. It has been said, humorously, that a woman is afraid that her husband won't change and a man is afraid that his wife will. If you can accept your partner exactly as he or she is, and let her know that you do, it will eliminate much of the stress in your life together. In such an atmosphere trust develops and love blossoms.

DAY 11

TRY THIS

Tell your partner
that your love
doesn't depend
upon what they do
or don't do.
And mean it!

TRY THIS

Talk together about how your sexual life can be loving and
mutually fulfilling.

Sexuality and Intimacy

Sexual attraction is one of the strongest forces in the world and the way you handle sex in your marriage will help determine whether or not your life together is fulfilling. Your sexual interaction should be a strong bonding element. But, if allowed to become a cause of tension, unsatisfying physical relationships can lead to divorce. Talk together about your sex life, about what it is and what you would like it to be. A little bit of communication in this area will go a long way toward creating a happy marriage. As you bring a greater feeling of love and tenderness into your physical relationship you will experience a deepening sense of true intimacy. Overindulgence in sex gradually erodes love and intimacy. Yet a sense of repression is to be avoided too. Find a balance that works for you, one that helps deepen your love for each other.

Happiness Is Within

Happiness is a state of mind. It grows from within. Possessions can't produce it nor does it come because some self-created condition has finally been met. Realize that you alone create or destroy your own happiness. When you accept this simple fact, then you and your partner can decide to have a happy life together regardless of events and conditions. Visualize happiness as a force field that surrounds you. Don't let anyone or anything weaken it. Inner happiness is contagious and will help lift your partner out of the quicksand of gloom. Happiness is also the breeding ground for other good qualities such as patience and understanding. It starts with a flow of positive energy, and often the best way to deal with the minor problems of life and marriage is to simply do something positive. A hug is worth a thousand words.

TRY THIS

Decide to build a bubble of happiness around your life together.

TRY THIS

Walk through your home with your partner. Look at colors, space, and appliances, in terms of how they influence your mood. Make changes to improve your environment.

Your Home
Environment

The environment in your home is more important than you might think. Our surroundings strongly influence our thoughts; our minds expand and relax in harmonious settings while depressing environments bring dark moods. A cluttered home indicates a cluttered mind while a clean light room brings a subtle sense of peace and order to your life. Don't fill your home with meaningless noise. For many couples the television is almost like having another person in the house, and an intrusive one at that! Consider putting yours out of the way in a location where it doesn't dominate your space. Subtle environmental influences will affect your marriage in surprisingly powerful ways. Visualize a place where you're happy and content. What colors predominate? What shapes are there? Do you hear the sound of music or running water? Try to recreate this feeling of harmony and peace in your home.

Live with Contentment

Contentment has been called the highest virtue. It comes from accepting things as they are rather than pushing them away because life isn't giving you exactly what you want. Discontentment is a disease of the heart that all the world's wealth cannot cure any more than an ocean of salt water can slake a raging thirst. Your true wealth is measured, not by the size of your bank account, but by the degree of your contentment. Contentment cannot be bought at any price, but it can be plucked for free from a thankful heart. If, today, you choose contentment as your constant companion, no one can take it from you. Here is an affirmation to help you wrap yourself in a shield of contentment:

I am grateful for my life exactly as it is.

I am thankful for this day.

I welcome every hour.

Thank you God.

Thank you God.

TRY THIS

Repeat this
affirmation
whenever you feel
the ripples of
discontentment.

By returning
daily to your own
center, you will
gather the strength
you need to face
all of life's
demands.

Keep Your
Marriage Creative

To keep your marriage creative, find new things to do together and perform familiar activities in new and different ways. Creative thinking draws a flow of energy from the very universe around us. This universal flow of creativity is the true source of great works by the geniuses of music, art, and science. View your marriage as a kind of art form. Don't let weeks or months pass while your relationship grows stagnant and boring. You can develop the habit of creativity by doing small things in new ways, like the way you cook a meal or spend a weekend. Creativity's flow is strongest when positive energy is high and is killed by criticism and passivity. Support your partner's creative endeavors even if they don't include you. His or her happiness will be your reward. Active pastimes may seem to demand energy, but they actually give you a much greater sense of relaxation than passive diversions such as watching TV. And co-creating something with your partner will help deepen your union in magical ways.

16 DAY

TRY THIS

Keep your energy high and creativity flowing. Plan to do a project or an activity that you've never done before. Think "outside the box."

TRY THIS

Make a small
decision, about a
meal or a movie,
where you both
cooperate equally
in the outcome.
It will be good
practice for
making important
decisions.

How To Make Decisions

There is no single "right" way to make decisions. But it is important that both of you feel that you have a say in what is decided. Don't let your marriage develop uneven power relationships where one partner makes all the important decisions. Naturally, one partner may have more influence in those areas where his or her expertise is more developed, but be sure to balance it with areas in which the other partner has a greater say. Important decisions need the active approval of both partners. Never make momentous decisions under the influence of strong, especially negative, emotions. Wait until you can get centered and calm. For important decisions, it is helpful to meditate or pray. Bring your intuition into play also. When you don't know which decision is right, mentally offer up different alternatives and see which course of action feels right. For intuition to work, you must remain calm and objective. When you're stuck, be willing to seek advice from those whom you respect and have more experience than you. Once you arrive at a decision, give it your full support.

Get Centered

Marriage, like life, must have a center to which it returns in order to gather strength. One of the most bonding practices a couple can do is to meditate together. There are many books to guide you, including my own, *How to Meditate*. Meditation is very simple. Here is a meditation to help your marriage. Sit together in a quiet place and relax your body. Then relax your mind by releasing all thoughts of past and future. Gaze calmly at the point between the eyebrows. From that point, simply observe the breath going in and out. When you are calm and centered, feel a warm glow of love starting in the area of your heart and then gradually spreading throughout your whole being. Now envelop your partner in that glow. Using your love as a "carrier wave" send thoughts of blessing and strength to your loved-one. If any tensions exist between you, let them dissolve in the waves of love. By returning daily to your own center, you will gather the strength you need to face all of life's demands.

TRY THIS

Meditate together.

19
DAY

TRY THIS

Be secure within yourself.

Security Is a
State of Mind

Security issues are something that all couples face. Serious problems may arise concerning finances, or health, or your relationship. Learn to face life's challenges constructively and to find your security within yourself. Be practical, but realize also that many things in life are beyond your control. Worrying won't change the outcome; it is just wasted energy that could be used to find solutions. Nothing you can do will give you total security. A man, foreseeing the start of World War II, decided to move to a safe, secure corner of the world. He chose, as the safest place on earth, the island of Guam! True security is a state of mind that can only be found within. And only you can provide it for yourself. Don't give your partner the impossible burden of being responsible for your own sense of security. Have faith in life and gratitude for whatever comes.

Develop Positive Magnetism

A marriage needs to develop positive magnetism. Human magnetism is surprisingly similar to its physical counterpart. Just as electricity flowing through a wire creates a magnetic field, so also a flow of energy creates a magnetic relationship. In people, however, the magnetism can be either positive or negative depending on the qualities of the thoughts and actions. Magnetism is a powerful although subtle force and you and your partner will attract people and opportunities according to the quality of the magnetism you put out. Positive, friendly, uplifted thoughts and actions will draw people of the same "vibration" to you. As they say, "Birds of a feather flock together." As a couple, be aware of the quality of your thoughts and interactions, including your subconscious patterns. Keep them positive and you will find that your relationship develops positive magnetism.

TRY THIS

Say yes to life! It will infuse your marriage with positive magnetism.

If you and your partner develop the simple habit of expressing appreciation, your marriage will take on a golden glow of harmony.

Life Is a Mirror

What do you want from your spouse — love, friendship, respect, appreciation? The surest way to get what you want is to give it to others! Life is a mirror that reflects back to us our attitudes and behavior. Have you ever noticed how much friendlier people are when you treat them as a friend? Test this principle the next time you go into a store. Treat the clerk like an old friend and see what happens. Understanding that life mirrors back your attitudes is vital to your marriage. Treat your spouse the way you want him or her to treat you. A giving heart not only expresses love but also draws it from others. You may not see the results immediately, but in the long run giving to your partner what you want for yourself will become the bedrock of your marriage. This simple principle lies at the heart of all the world's religions. As Jesus stated it in the golden rule, "Do unto others as you would have them do unto you."

DAY 21

TRY THIS

Observe how people reflect back to you the same kind of energy
you give to them.

D A Y

22

TRY THIS

Set your mind to do something that stretches you a bit.

Then do it!

The Power of
the Will

One of the strongest forces in the universe is the power of the will — energy directed toward a goal. Most people have not developed even a tiny portion of the potential of their will-power. You and your partner can accomplish anything you want as long as you stay committed to your goal. Never accept defeat. Even if you fail, don't admit that you've been defeated. Say rather, "We just haven't succeeded yet." Winston Churchill once was very late for a graduation talk he was to give. His whole speech to the student body consisted of, "Never give up. Never ever give up. Never ever, ever give up!" One way to develop will power is to take on a small task and make sure to accomplish it. Then, successively, take on more difficult projects, always being certain you finish them. Gradually you will become convinced that you can accomplish whatever you decide to do. When you and your partner combine the power of your individual wills, you can create a force that nothing in the world can stop.

Take Control of Habits

Habits can be your greatest allies or your greatest enemies. Take an inventory of the patterns you have developed in your relationship. Do you habitually support each other or have you begun to complain and criticize? Do you regularly do activities together that strengthen you marriage or have you fallen into unfulfilling routines? At the beginning of each year we traditionally make resolutions, giving up a bad habit or starting a good one. Today, make a "New Year's resolution" for your marriage. Habits often take time to change, they obey the law of momentum. Old ones stay in place until we put out the energy needed to change them. It can take considerable effort in the beginning to change an old habit, but every day becomes easier. One of the best ways to drop a bad habit is to introduce a positive one to replace it, one that is the opposite of the old. Let compliments replace criticism. Let energy replace laziness. Occasionally review the habits that have developed in your marriage. Throw out some unwanted ones and bring in something positive.

TRY THIS

Take inventory of the habits that have crept into your relationship and discard the unwanted ones.

TRY THIS

Think high thoughts and do high deeds.

Be High-minded

No relationship will be truly satisfying unless it expresses high thoughts and attitudes. Our souls crave goodness, and we won't flourish unless high-minded thoughts are part of our mental diet. Spend a little time reading together the writings of the great thinkers, especially those you consider to be wise or saintly. Then be active, not passive, and try to incorporate some of their ideas into your life. Spend, also, a little time each day thinking about how you can help others. Then act on your thoughts. Make your marriage a beacon of light for others. If you bless the world through your actions, you will find that the world blesses you in turn. Each day commune with your own highest self through prayer or meditation. High-mindedness will create an umbrella of grace over you and your partner where the rains of pettiness can't reach.

DAY 24

Live in Harmony

Harmony is a sign that things are going well with your marriage. Be sure to nurture and protect it. It is said that in ancient China the wise ruler listened first to the music in his provinces. If the music was harmonious he knew the district was being well run. Make harmony one of the high principles in your life together. If you both seek harmony, even disagreements can be resolved in such a way that they strengthen a marriage. Never go to bed mad at your partner. The natural antidote to anger is not more anger, but patience and understanding. One moment of patience in a time of great stress can build a deep bond of understanding, while the whiplash of impatience in the same situation can begin to unravel the very fabric of your relationship. Dwelling on problems usually just makes them grow. It is much better to work harmoniously together to find positive solutions. And never lose your sense of humor. A good shared laugh will help restore balance to your marriage.

TRY THIS

Let your partner know, through words and actions, that harmony
is of utmost importance to you.

Be happy

under all

circumstances.

Subtle
Communication

We communicate in many ways beyond mere speech. Body language, facial expression, even our posture sends instant messages to those around us. The subtle signals you send your partner are often more important than your words. When you are talking together, look at her and pay attention. To continue with an activity sends the silent message, "What you have to say isn't important to me." When you greet him, do so enthusiastically not absentmindedly. Your subtle communications, like the invisible air we breathe, create an atmosphere for your life together. On a deeper level, your very thoughts send messages to your partner. Many couples develop an almost eerie ability to know what the other one is thinking. Make sure that you are sending silent messages of love and support.

26

DAY

TRY THIS

Become aware
of the messages
in your
non-verbal
communication.

TRY THIS

Forgive all the hurts your partner may have given you.

Start fresh from this moment on.

Forgive
and Forget

Sometimes in a marriage it is best to have a poor memory. Don't hold on to old

disappointments and hurts. The ability to forgive and forget lets you start each

day fresh. We can keep our partner trapped in a cage by holding on to negative

thoughts and expectations. Is anything more important than your love for each

other? Sometimes it is difficult to express forgiveness in words. If so, feel it in your

heart and express it in your actions. Later you can talk about it. Don't allow your

mind to dwell on old issues. When past hurts arise, replace them immediately

with thoughts of healing, forgiveness and appreciation. As a couple, forgive those

who may have hurt you. Send silent blessings to help heal whatever it is that

made them act in hurtful ways. One of the clearest signs of a well-integrated

person is the ability to forgive others.

Watch the
Longer Rhythms

Life is built a day at a time and the minutes are more important than the years.
But, remember, the long-term outcome is more important than short-term results.
Each action, like grains of sand in an hourglass, gradually adds to the total of
your life. The patterns of your daily interactions will become powerful influences
over time. Think about what qualities your present patterns will produce in five
or ten years. Your marriage is like a tree — it can be trained to be healthy and
beautiful. Now is the time to establish the "personality" you want for your life
together. Train yourselves to express the traits that will help your marriage grow
strong and beautiful. Make a list of the five qualities that you would most like
to see expressed in your life together. Then make sure that you nourish them with
daily repetition.

28 DAY

TRY THIS

Have a
conversation
about what you
would like your
marriage
to be in ten
years.

TRY THIS

Help one person in need. Then talk about how your marriage can bring light to others.

Expansive
Consciousness

Expand your sympathies to include the good of everyone. Expansive consciousness means that you are able to feel the needs of others. Too much thinking about yourself will harden your heart and cloud your mind. Pain is the inevitable result of excessive self-focus. It is so simple to overcome this tendency. Help others! Accept, also, the fact that your partner's needs are as important as your own. Start by making life better for your family but don't stop there. Think of ways that your marriage can be a gift to others. Make your home a haven for your friends and loved ones, a place where they can always find friendship and support. Then expand beyond those you know personally. Find ways to help other people, to heal the environment, to bring balance and harmony to this fragile planet. One of the best ways for a couple to strengthen their bond is to do volunteer service together. Time spent in this way connects you to your higher self, to the higher self of your partner, and to all life around you.

Evaluate Your Marriage

It is a good practice to mentally review each day before you go to sleep. Be objective when you look at your reactions to the day's events, as if you were reviewing the actions of a close friend. Take time to analyze your relationship in this way. What are its strong points, its weaknesses? Is it headed in the direction you want? Each of you should decide independently what you need to work on in yourself. Then together, talk about what you need to improve in your marriage. Does it need more levity, more enthusiasm, more gratitude? Look back through the topics in this book and see what strikes you. But, don't be hard on yourselves. Life is for enjoyment. Enjoy each other and find joy in your union.

30

TRY THIS

Review your
marriage
and make sure
it is headed
where you
want it to go.

Have faith
in life, and
gratitude for
whatever comes.

Other titles in the 30-Day Essentials series:

30-Day Essentials for Career by Jyotish Novak

30-Day Essentials for Health & Healing by Jyotish Novak

Also by Jyotish Novak

How to Meditate: A Step-by-Step Guide to the Art and Science of Meditation

Meditation Therapy for Relationships (video)

Meditation Therapy for Stress & Change (video)

Meditation Therapy for Health & Healing (video)

Additional books from Crystal Clarity Publishers

Expansive Marriage: A Way to Self-Realization by J. Donald Walters

Secrets of Love by J. Donald Walters

Secrets of Happiness by J. Donald Walters